RANDY'S CORNER

DAY BY DAY WITH...

# CARRIE UNDERWOOD

BY
RISA BROWN

## Mitchell Lane
PUBLISHERS

P.O. Box 196
Hockessin, Delaware 19707
Visit us on the web: www.mitchelllane.com
Comments? Email us:
mitchelllane@mitchelllane.com

**Mitchell Lane**
PUBLISHERS

Printing     1       2       3       4       5       6       7       8       9

# RANDY'S CORNER

## DAY BY DAY WITH. . .

| | |
|---|---|
| Adam Jones | Justin Bieber |
| Alex Morgan | LeBron James |
| Beyoncé | Manny Machado |
| Bindi Sue Irwin | Mia Hamm |
| Calvin Johnson | Miley Cyrus |
| Carrie Underwood | Missy Franklin |
| Chloë Moretz | Selena Gomez |
| Dwayne "The Rock" Johnson | Shaun White |
| Elena Delle Donne | Stephen Hillenburg |
| Eli Manning | Taylor Swift |
| Gabby Douglas | Willow Smith |

Library of Congress Cataloging-in-Publication Data
Brown, Risa W., author.
 Day by day with Carrie Underwood / by Risa Brown.
    pages cm. — (Randy's corner)
 Includes bibliographical references and index.
 ISBN 978-1-61228-631-0 (library bound)
 1.  Underwood, Carrie, 1983– —Juvenile literature. 2.  Singers—United States—
Biography—Juvenile literature.  I. Title.
 ML3930.U53B76 2014
 782.421642092—dc23
 [B]
                                                                      2014008306

eBook ISBN: 97816912286570

**ABOUT THE AUTHOR:** Risa Brown is the author of twelve books for children and three for librarians. She was a children's or school librarian for twenty-three years. She now writes full-time and lives in Arlington, Texas. She sings in a community chorus and loves to travel.

**PUBLISHER'S NOTE:** The following story has been thoroughly researched and to the best of our knowledge represents a true story. While every possible effort has been made to ensure accuracy, the publisher will not assume liability for damages caused by inaccuracies in the data and makes no warranty on the accuracy of the information contained herein.

PBP

# DAY BY DAY WITH CARRIE UNDERWOOD

Carrie Underwood is a country music Cinderella. She went from being a college student to a star, thanks to *American Idol.*

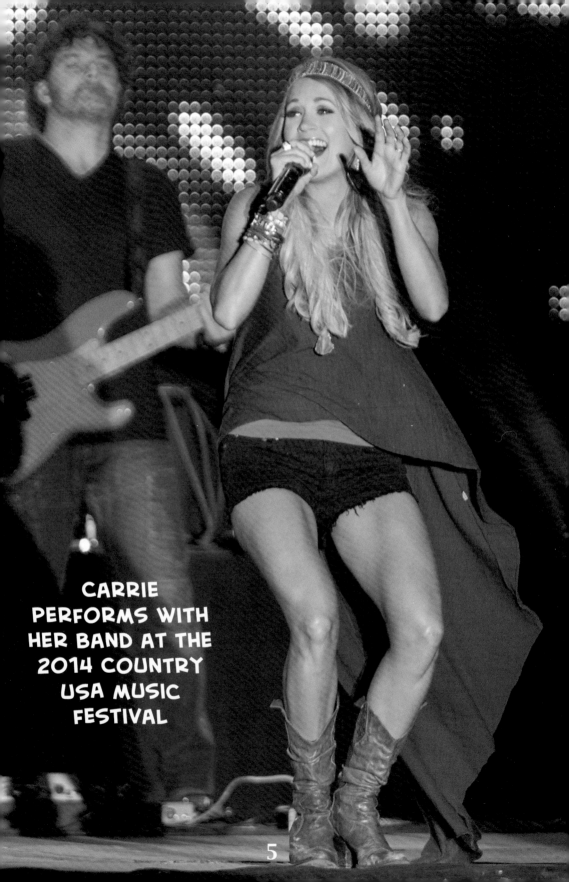

CARRIE PERFORMS WITH HER BAND AT THE 2014 COUNTRY USA MUSIC FESTIVAL

**6**

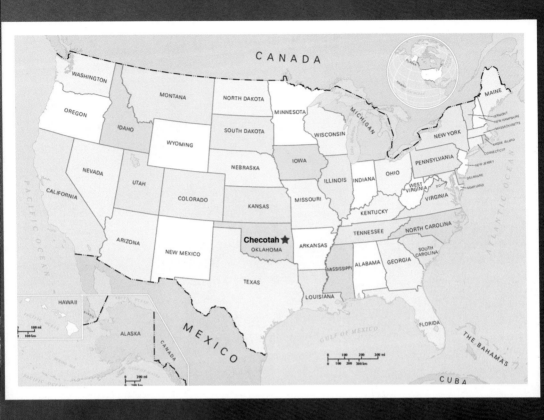

Carrie Marie Underwood was born on March 10, 1983. She grew up on a farm in Oklahoma in a town called Checotah. Carrie loved to play with the animals on her farm.

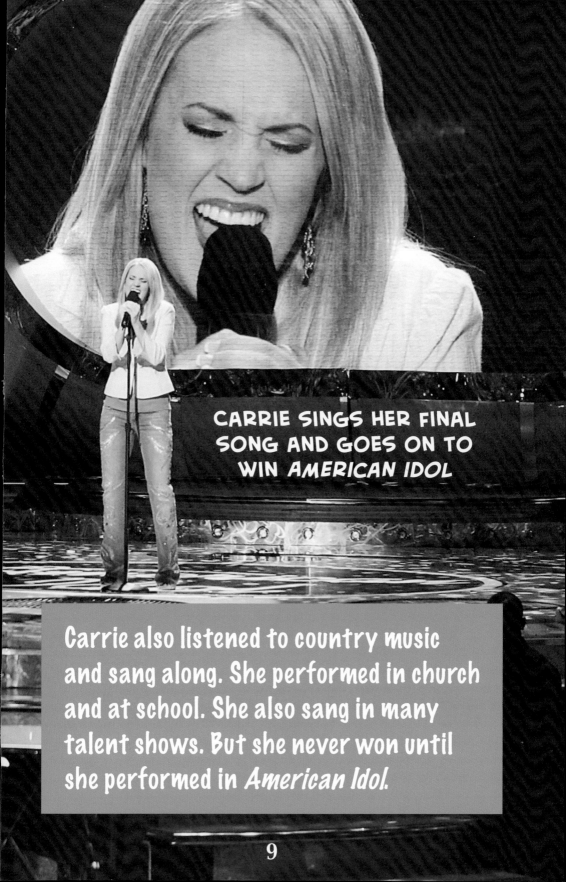

CARRIE SINGS HER FINAL SONG AND GOES ON TO WIN *AMERICAN IDOL*

Carrie also listened to country music and sang along. She performed in church and at school. She also sang in many talent shows. But she never won until she performed in *American Idol.*

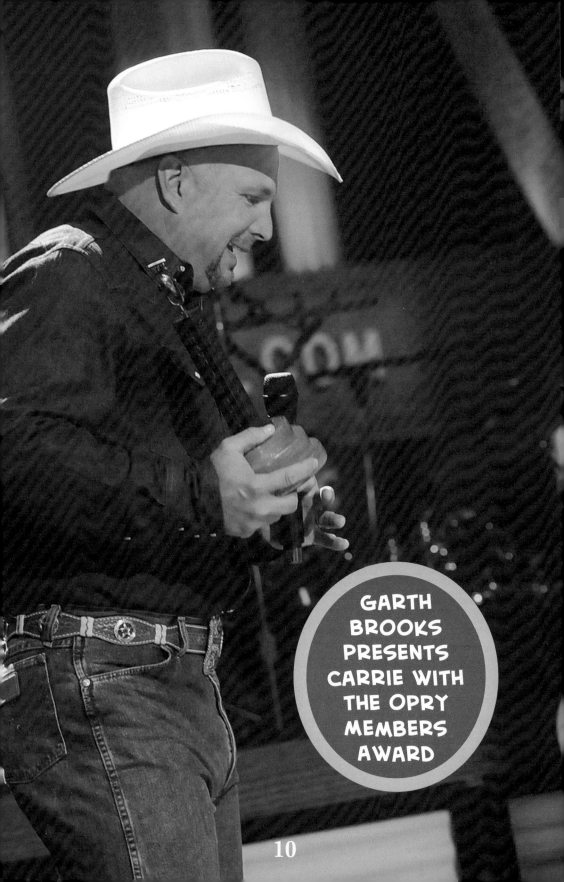

GARTH BROOKS PRESENTS CARRIE WITH THE OPRY MEMBERS AWARD

After *American Idol,* Carrie moved to Nashville to record her first album. Her fans loved her songs and she has won many awards. Carrie was inducted into the Grand Ole Opry in 2008.

BRAD
PAISLEY

Since 2008, Carrie has also hosted the Country Music Association award show each year with Brad Paisley. Country music

BRAD AND
CARRIE
PERFORM
DURING THE
45TH ANNUAL
CMA AWARDS

fans love Carrie. But she has brought new
fans to country music, too.

At first Carrie was not sure she could write songs but she wanted to try. Now she works with a team to write many of the songs that she sings on her albums.

A YOUNG FAN SINGS WITH CARRIE

Carrie travels the world to meet her fans and perform songs from her albums. She admits she used to be afraid when so many people wanted to get near her. Now she takes extra time to spend with her fans.

CARRIE POSES WITH A COUPLE OF FANS

Carrie met Mike Fisher in 2008. He was a hockey player for the Ottawa Senators. They got married in 2010 and Mike now plays for the Nashville Predators.

MIKE FISHER (#12) OF THE NASHVILLE PREDATORS

Carrie's parents still live in Checotah in the house where Carrie grew up. They did not let Carrie buy them a new house. Carrie's mom Carole is a retired teacher. Steve, Carrie's dad, worked in a paper mill. She has two older sisters.

STEVE
UNDERWOOD
(FATHER)

Carrie wears beautiful dresses on stage but she says her favorite thing to wear is a hoodie.

Carrie loves animals. When she was thirteen, she became a vegetarian because she did not want to eat animals. She supports many animal organizations such as the Humane Society. Carrie has two dogs, named Ace and Pennie. She starts each day by taking her dogs out in the morning.

CARRIE ATTENDS THE 6TH ANNUAL
PEDIGREE ADOPTION DRIVE

CARRIE'S
DOG
"ACE"

Carrie supports organizations that help children such as Save the Children and St. Jude Children's Research Hospital. Carrie sang "Just Stand Up!" with other famous singers to raise money for cancer research. She also gave $1 million to the American Red Cross after tornadoes hit Oklahoma.

CARRIE UNDERWOOD AND CITY OF HOPE CANCER SURVIVOR JOHN CLOER

CARRIE UP TO BAT DURING A SOFTBALL GAME TO RAISE MONEY FOR KIDS WITH CANCER.

Carrie is now acting in movies and on television. She had a part in the film *Soul Surfer* in 2011. In 2013, she played Maria von Trapp in the musical *The Sound of Music Live!* which was shown on NBC.

CARRIE HOLDS HER AWARDS FOR ENTERTAINER OF THE YEAR AND TOP FEMALE VOCALIST OF THE YEAR

Those who know Carrie Underwood say she is a hard worker. She hopes that she can continue to work hard and sing for a long time. But she told *Behind the Music,* "If it all ended tomorrow, I'm so blessed and so happy for everything that I've gotten to do."

**CARRIE SIGNS AUTOGRAPHS**

# FURTHER READING

## FIND OUT MORE

Bodden, Valerie. *Carrie Underwood*. Mankato, MN: Creative Education, 2014.

Brooks, Riley. *Carrie Underwood, American Dream/Hunter Hayes, A Dream Come True*. New York: Scholastic, 2013.

Burns, Kylie. *Carrie Underwood*. St. Catharines, Canada: Crabtree Publishing, 2013.

## WORKS CONSULTED

Effron, Lauren. "Carrie Underwood's 5 Must-Haves While on Tour." ABC News, April 25, 2012. http://abcnews.go.com/blogs/entertainment/2012/04/carrie-underwoods-5-must-haves-while-on-tour/

E!Online website. "'The Sound of Music Live!' Stars Tell All." http://www.eonline.com/videos/215847/the-sound-of-music-live-stars-tell-all

Glock, Allison. "Full Disclosure." *Marie Claire*, June 2013, pp. 139-146.

Halperin, Shirley. "Carrie: Success Is the Best Revenge." *Teen People*, September 2006, p. 38. MasterFile Premier.

Hearst Communication. "Marie Claire June 2013 Cover Star: Carrie Underwood Video." *Marie Claire* website. http://www.marieclaire.com/video/marie-claire-june-2013-cover-star-carrie-underwood-video-2341176110001

Look to the Stars. "Carrie Underwood: Charity Work, Events and Causes." https://www.looktothestars.org/celebrity/carrie-underwood

VH1. "Carrie Underwood." *Behind the Music*, October 2, 2012. http://www.vh1.com/video/behind-the-music/full-episodes/behind-the-music-carrie-underwood/1694742/playlist.jhtml

## ON THE INTERNET

Billboard: Carrie Underwood http://www.billboard.com/artist/298758/carrie-underwood

Bio.: Carrie Underwood Biography http://www.biography.com/people/carrie-underwood-16730308

Grand Ole Opry: Carrie Underwood http://www.opry.com/artist/carrie-underwood

Official Carrie Underwood Website http://www.carrieunderwoodofficial.com/us/home

# INDEX